D0065772

A Gift

For:

From:

EAT less cottage cheese and more ICE CREAM

Thoughts on Life from Erma Bombeck

GIFT BOOKS
from Hallmark

Andrews McMeel Publishing®

BOK2046

This edition published in 2003 by Andrews McMeel Publishing exclusively for Hallmark Cards, Inc.

www.hallmark.com

ISBN: 0-7407-4367-8

Illustrations by Lynn Chang

The text of this book originally appeared in a newspaper column, "If I Had My Life To Live Over," on December 2, 1979.

EAT less cottage cheese and more ICE CREAM

Someone asked me **the other day** *if I had my life to live over,* would I change anything.

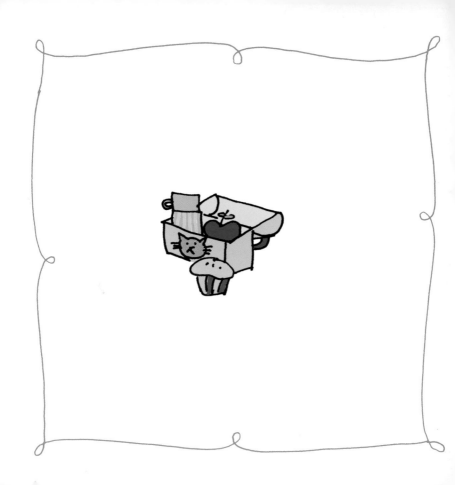

My answer was no, but then I *thought* about it and **changed** my mind.

If I had to
live my life
over again
I would have
waxed less
and
listened more.

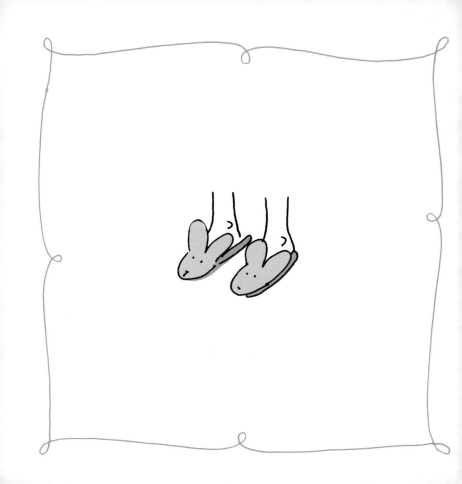

*Instead of
wishing away
nine months
of pregnancy and
complaining about
the shadow over my feet,
I'd have cherished every minute
of it and realized that the wonderment
growing inside me was to be my only
chance in life to assist **God** in a miracle.*

I would never have
insisted the car windows
be rolled up on a summer day
because my hair had just been
teased and SPRAYED.

I would have invited
friends over to
dinner even if the
carpet was **stained**
and the sofa faded.

I would have eaten

popcorn in the "**good**"

living room and

worried **less** about

the dirt when

you lit the

fireplace.

I would have taken the time to listen to my grandfather ramble about his youth.

I would have burnt
the *pink* candle
that was sculptured
like a rose before it
melted in storage.

I would
have sat
CROSS-LEGGED

on the lawn
with my children
and never worried
about grass stains.

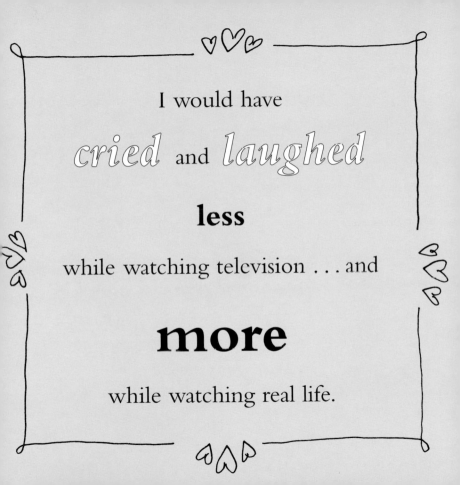

I would have

cried and *laughed*

less

while watching television . . . and

more

while watching real life.

I would
have shared
more of the
responsibility
carried by
my husband.

I would have eaten less
cottage cheese
and more
ice cream.

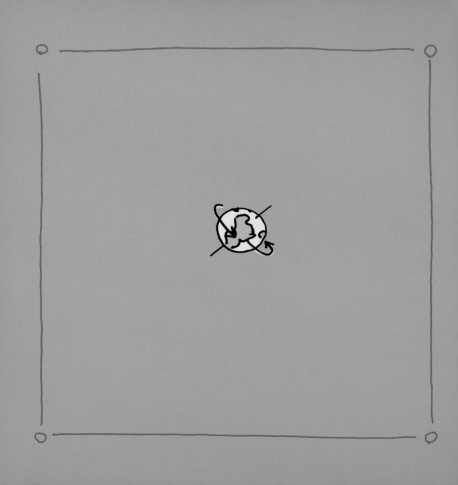

I would have **gone to** **bed** when I was **sick** instead of *pretending*  the Earth would go into a holding pattern if I weren't there for a day.

I would
never have
bought *anything*
just because it
was practical/wouldn't
show soil/guaranteed
to last a lifetime.

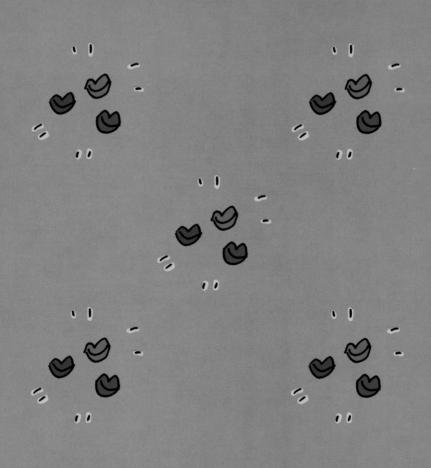

When my child kissed me

impetuously,

I would never have said,

"Later.

Now go get washed up for dinner."

There would
have been more
I love yous . . .
more I'm sorrys . . .
more I'm listenings . . .

but **mostly,**

given another shot

at *life,*

I would seize
every minute of it . . .

look at it

and

really

see

it . . .

try it on ...

live it ...

exhaust it ...

and

never

give that minute back

until there was

nothing left

of it.